beko
adidas
UTRERA
IRST N

A Pillar Box Red Publication

in association with

ISBN: 978-1-907823-74-9

BARCELONA ANNUAL 2017

Written by
James Bandy & Jamie Evans

Designed by
Calum Booth & Stuart Garneys

CONTENTS

NEYMAR JR
11
unicef

SEASON REVIEW

With records broken, trophies won and rivals conquered, it's been another remarkable chapter in the story of FC Barcelona...

AUGUST

DID YOU KNOW?
Barça have now won the Super Cup five times – more than any other team!

For Luis Enrique and his team, the season kicked off with the UEFA Super Cup against Sevilla. Barça's highest-scoring game of the season started badly when they fell behind inside three minutes, before goals from Lionel Messi (twice), Rafinha and Luis Suarez put the Catalans 4-1 up and in charge.
But the trophy was far from safe, and the Europa League holders produced an incredible comeback in the second half to take the game into extra-time. With the players tiring, Enrique turned to bundle-of-energy Pedro, and he didn't disappoint. The forward struck a dramatic winner with what would be his last goal for the club before joining Chelsea.
After a long flight home, Barça slumped to a 4-0 defeat at Athletic Bilbao in the first leg of the Spanish Super Cup, and any hope of a comeback in the second leg was ended by a Pique red card.
They didn't have to wait long for revenge, though. Returning to Bilbao for the opening day of La Liga, a Suarez volley secured a 1-0 win, and a week later Thomas Vermaelen was celebrating his first La Liga goal at home to Malaga as the club made a 100% start to their title defence.

SEPTEMBER

Following the birth of his son, Barça went to Atletico Madrid for the first major test of their title defence without Messi, who was on the subs' bench. With the scores level after an hour, Luis Enrique turned to his super-sub and, sure enough, on came Leo to fire in the winner, and give his team a crucial three points. Days later, the Champions League holders were denied an opening win in their first European game of the season by an incredible strike by Roma's Alessandro Florenzi in a 1-1 draw,

STAT ATTACK!

Messi played his 100th Champions League game in the match at Roma!

before a 4-1 win at home to Levante kept them top of La Liga after four games. However, the positive start wouldn't last. A devastating performance from ex-Barça winger Nolito fired Celta Vigo to a shock 4-1 win, before disaster struck in the home match against Las Palmas: an injury to Messi.

OCTOBER

Life without Leo started badly for Barça. With Sandro Munir called up as his replacement, the Catalans travelled to Sevilla for Matchday Seven. A Neymar penalty wasn't enough to prevent a 2-1 defeat, but it didn't take them long to bounce back. Neymar and Suarez each scored La Liga hat-tricks either side of a 2-0 win over BATE in the Champions League, before a 2-0 win at Getafe kept them joint-top of La Liga with ten games played.

NOVEMBER

STAT ATTACK!

Suarez and Neymar scored 18 goals in just eight games while Messi was injured!

By the first Clasico of the season, at the Bernabeu on November 21, Barça were flying. Impressive 3-0 wins over BATE and Villarreal gave them plenty of confidence, even with the returning Messi only fit enough for the bench. Suarez and Neymar continued their red-hot form with a goal each in the first half, before Iniesta killed off the game on 53 minutes. Victory was already in the bag when Messi came on shortly afterwards, although there was still time for Suarez to make it 4-0 and send Barça six points clear at the top of La Liga. The victory proved inspirational, as a 6-1 win over Roma a couple of days later sent them into the second round of the Champions League as group winners, before another dominant 4-0 win against Real Sociedad the following weekend kept their title bid on track.

DECEMBER

DID YOU KNOW?

Suarez is the joint top goalscorer in Club World Cup history!

After thrashing Vilanovense 6-1 in the Copa del Rey, and consecutive draws with Valencia, Bayer Leverkusen and Deportivo, Barça headed off to Japan for the Club World Cup.

In the first game, a Suarez hat-trick against Guangzhou Evergrande inspired them to a comfortable victory and set up a final with River Plate.

Once again, the Uruguayan was in top form, bagging two more goals after a Messi opener to give Barça their fifth trophy of 2015.

The year was wrapped up in style ten days later. Messi celebrated his 500th game in a blue and red shirt by scoring in a 4-0 win over Real Betis, keeping his team in the title hunt going into 2016.

The new year began with three games in 11 days against local rivals Espanyol. After a 0-0 draw away from home, Barça ran out 4-1 winners in the first leg of the Copa del Rey, as Messi set a new record for goals in the derby. Aleix Vidal and Arda Turan finally got to make their debuts too, months after signing.

Another 4-0 win, this time against Granada, was sandwiched between the second leg of the Cup, with a 2-0 victory securing Barça's sixth straight quarter final appearance.

In La Liga, Barça continued to pile pressure on Atletico Madrid. A 6-0 win at home to Athletic Bilbao was followed by a 2-1 win at Malaga, leaving them level on points with their title rivals ahead of a crucial meeting at the Nou Camp. Atleti opened the scoring through Koke, but their lead did not last long. Goals from Messi and Suarez put Barça back in control before half time, before red cards for Filipe Luis and Diego Godin killed off any chance of a comeback. The victory moved the holders three points clear at the top of La Liga with a game in hand, making them favourites to retain their crown.

FEBRUARY

The first visitors to the Nou Camp in February were Valencia, for the first leg of the Copa del Rey semi final. It proved to be one of the best performances of the season, as Gary Neville's side were stunned 7-0 thanks to a hat-trick from Messi and four from Luis Suarez.

Their outstanding form continued in the league, winning every game in February, before ending the month with a trip to Arsenal in the Champions League. In a tight contest at The Emirates, Messi made the difference. He broke the deadlock on 71 minutes following a rapid counter-attack, before adding another crucial away goal from the penalty spot 12 minutes later. Barça looked on course for another quarter-final spot.

MARCH

With a haul of 15 goals in three games at the start of the month – including six from Messi – Barcelona extended their lead at the top of La Liga to eight points. They looked unstoppable as they welcomed Arsenal to the Nou Camp for the second leg of their Round Of 16 Champions League tie. The English club caused few problems, as goals from each of Barça's front three fired them to an impressive 3-1 victory.

But the league leaders were not so convincing the following weekend, as they threw away a two-goal lead at Villarreal to draw 2-2. Luis Enrique insisted that the game was a 'positive result', after defeat for Atletico Madrid gave his team a nine-point lead at the top of the table. However, results were about to get a lot worse.

STAT ATTACK!

The 2-2 draw at Villarreal ended Barça's 12-match winning streak!

APRIL

April started disastrously for Barcelona, as their 39-game unbeaten run was ended by Zinedine Zidane's Real Madrid. A late Cristiano Ronaldo goal delivered the sucker punch, and Real's first win at the Nou Camp since 2012.

Three days later, Barcelona welcomed Atletico for the Champions League quarter-final. The home fans feared the worst when Fernando Torres opened the scoring in the first half, only for the same player to be sent off ten minutes later. Two goals from Suarez sealed the comeback, but the tie was far from over.

Their shaky form continued in La Liga with a 1-0 defeat at Real Sociedad, before a trip to the Vicente Calderon for the second leg of their Champions League quarter-final with Atletico.

After a brace from Antoine Griezmann, Barça's dream of retaining the Champions League was dead. The following weekend, defeat at Valencia made it four games without a win, and the title race was back on.

But Barça responded in the best way possible. Once again, Suarez was on fire, scoring nine goals in three games as they ended the month with 8-0, 6-0 and 2-0 victories, which left them level on points with Atletico.

MAY

With their form restored, Barcelona went into another derby full of confidence. A stunning free-kick from Messi and a Suarez brace helped them on their way to 5-0 win, while results elsewhere meant that they only needed one more point to retain their title.
There were a few nerves as the team headed to Granada for Matchday 38, but Suarez was on hand to settle them with two goals in the first 45 minutes. After half-time, the ex-Liverpool man completed his hat-trick to spark wild celebrations. Now they could turn their attention to the Copa del Rey final.
After winning the Europa League just a few days previously, Sevilla were confident, especially after a first-half red card for Javier Mascherano. But in an end-to-end game, neither side could find a winner in normal time. The game swung back in the holders' favour in stoppage time when Banega was sent off for a cynical foul, and they finally took the leadin extra-time.
It took a moment of genius from Messi to carve open the Sevilla defence as he put Alba through on goal with an incredible through pass. The left-back made no mistake, poking the ball past Rico to put Barça in front. After a second Sevilla player saw red, Neymar wrapped the game up, finishing another brilliant pass from Messi. Barcelona had won the Copa del Rey for the 28th time.
Enrique ran on to the pitch to celebrate his seventh trophy in two years with his team, and summed up the final perfectly. "It has been a spectacular end to the season," he said. "This team is made up of champions."

DID YOU KNOW?

Barça have won more Copas del Rey (28), and more league and cup doubles (7), than any other team!

WORDSEARCH

Can you find the names of all these Barcelona legends?

E	U	Q	I	R	N	E	R	D	Q	V	A	L	D	E	S	P	L	J	M
R	X	O	H	N	I	D	L	A	N	O	R	L	L	K	G	O	Z	K	T
E	N	G	G	U	A	R	D	I	O	L	A	P	P	L	Y	B	Q	V	C
R	F	T	K	R	Q	T	K	Z	L	K	X	B	C	U	Z	C	J	K	P
R	B	T	D	P	I	M	K	L	R	K	J	R	P	E	R	N	Y	N	N
E	R	E	P	O	T	V	D	Z	U	H	E	Y	R	V	W	D	E	V	F
F	G	K	G	N	D	E	A	B	K	P	T	A	K	W	Y	E	U	Q	C
K	F	Q	R	I	C	L	A	L	M	L	U	M	L	K	S	K	L	A	N
W	W	O	D	O	R	L	A	A	D	S	U	B	A	K	E	R	O	R	L
G	M	G	C	W	A	I	G	N	Y	O	N	I	E	T	T	V	D	F	L
A	L	Q	R	N	J	P	S	Q	O	K	F	N	V	T	T	Q	T	Z	V
X	K	N	U	V	H	D	N	T	X	R	S	A	R	E	X	A	C	H	O
V	T	M	Y	D	T	L	H	W	A	T	Y	N	K	Z	R	P	Y	K	K
V	V	L	F	T	R	A	M	O	K	I	N	O	B	R	Y	T	L	O	H
X	I	D	F	B	P	D	N	T	O	J	N	D	K	O	J	W	K	E	C
A	L	L	R	P	T	I	R	L	R	T	T	A	H	M	D	T	N	M	I
V	F	X	L	T	R	B	J	T	V	B	E	R	R	A	L	F	N	A	O
I	R	R	V	A	R	A	F	M	F	M	L	A	Y	R	T	R	B	N	T
Z	U	B	I	Z	A	R	R	E	T	A	Y	M	Y	I	X	F	V	Z	S
G	V	Z	W	Y	N	O	S	S	R	A	L	B	R	O	N	W	Z	T	D

- Abidal
- Amor
- Bakero
- Begiristain
- Cruyff
- Deco
- Enrique
- Eto'o
- Ferrer
- Gamper
- Guardiola
- Kluivert
- Koeman
- Kubala
- Larsson
- Laudrup
- Maradona
- Neeskens
- Puyol
- Rexach
- Rivaldo
- Romario
- Ronaldinho
- Ronaldo
- Stoichkov
- Suarez
- Valdes
- Villa
- Xavi
- Zubizarreta

NAME THE TEAM

The stars from Barcelona's Champions League clash with Arsenal are hiding – can you work out who they are?

1. Goalkeeper
2. Centre-back
3. Centre-back
4. Centre midfield
5. Defensive midfield
6. Right wing

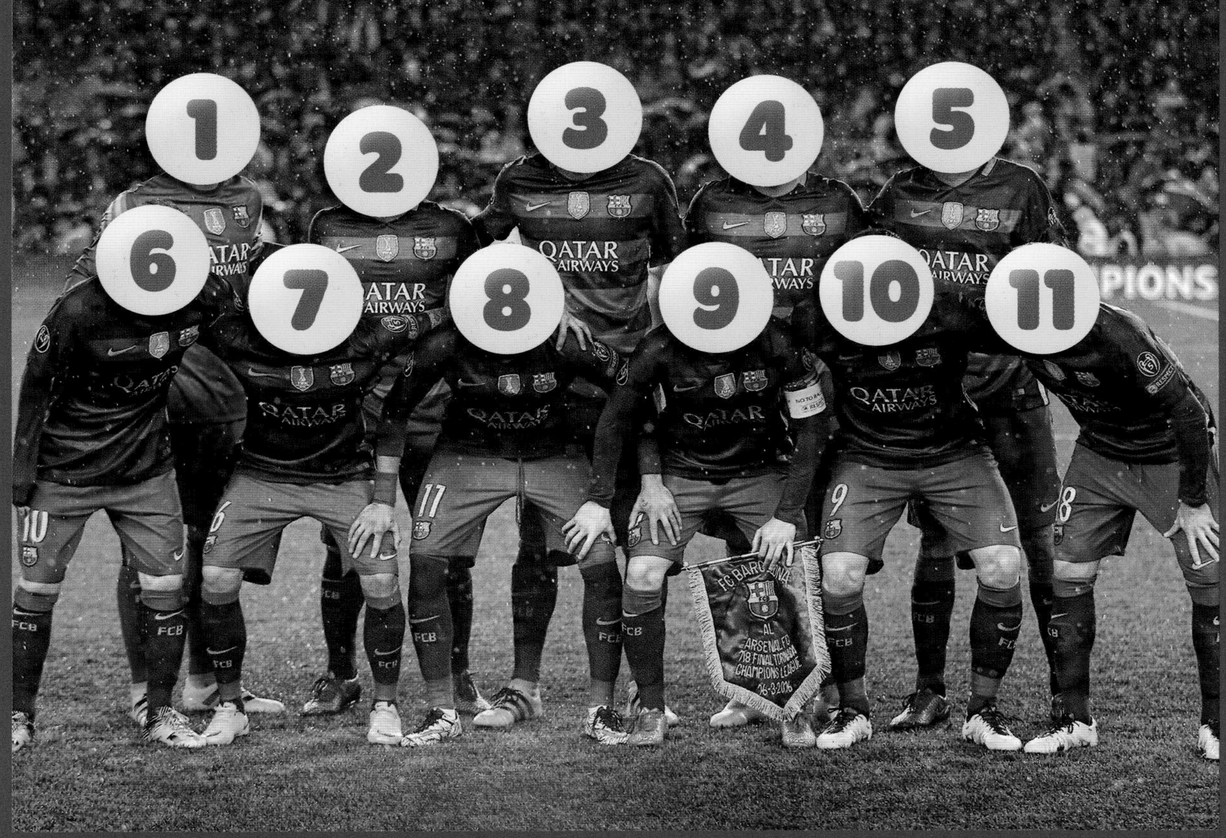

7. Right-back
8. Left wing
9. Centre midfield
10. Striker
11. Left-back

ANSWERS ON P60-61

MESSI SUAREZ NEYMAR

THE GREATEST STRIKEFORCE ON THE PLANET

If you asked football fans to name the three best forwards in world football, Lionel Messi, Luis Suarez and Neymar would be certain to feature heavily. So for all three superstars to play for the same club is a frightening prospect, not least for opposition defenders. Here we take a look at what makes each player so special, the stats that prove it, and how they work together to form the most devastating forward line in world football today...

QATAR AIRWAYS
NOW TURN OVER FOR MORE!

MESSI

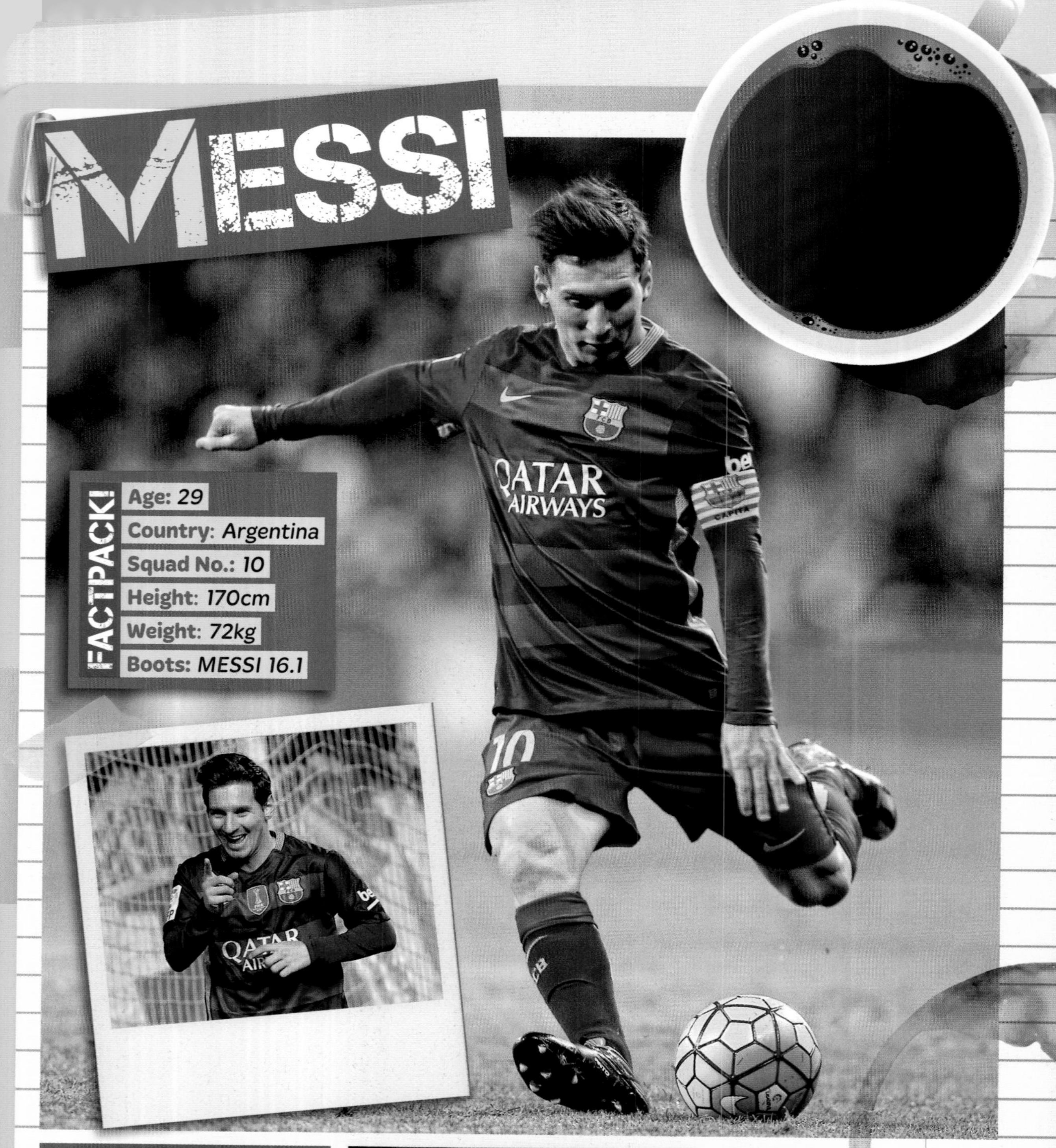

FACTPACK!

- **Age:** *29*
- **Country:** *Argentina*
- **Squad No.:** *10*
- **Height:** *170cm*
- **Weight:** *72kg*
- **Boots:** *MESSI 16.1*

Put simply, Messi has the lot. He dribbles like the ball is stuck to his foot and his low centre of gravity lets him change direction in an instant, which helps him create chances for Suarez and Neymar. Messi's lethal in front of goal, too – he can pass the ball into the net, but is just as happy hitting rocket shots.

MESSI'S STATS

Finishing	99
Headers	88
Power	85
Speed	89
Dribbling	95
Creativity	96
Long Shots	94
Tricks	91
Footy Brain	91

SUAREZ

FACTPACK!
Age: 29
Country: Uruguay
Squad No.: 9
Height: 182cm
Weight: 85kg
Boots: Adidas X

One of the Uruguayan's many strengths is his incredible work-rate, and the way he closes down defenders and makes unselfish runs off the ball creates chances for Messi and Neymar. But he's also incredible on the ball, has quick feet and great awareness, and is lethal in one-on-one positions.

SUAREZ'S STATS	
Finishing	93
Headers	86
Power	87
Speed	89
Dribbling	95
Creativity	96
Long Shots	94
Tricks	91
Footy Brain	91

NEYMAR

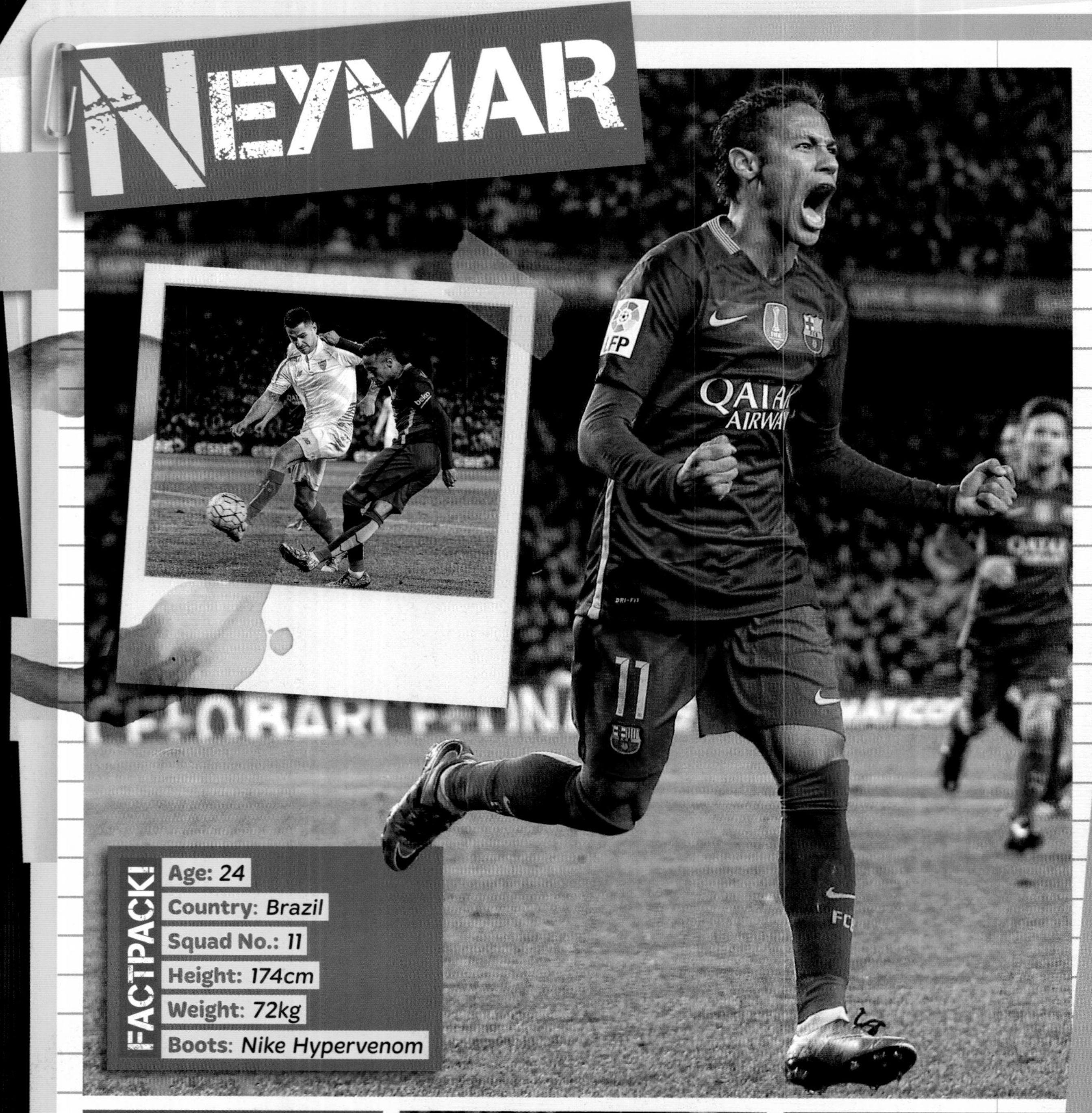

FACTPACK!

Age: 24
Country: Brazil
Squad No.: 11
Height: 174cm
Weight: 72kg
Boots: Nike Hypervenom

If Messi has the finishing and Suarez the workrate, then Neymar brings the unknown. The Brazilian is a maverick genius, capable of moments of outrageous skill. He is the master of the flip-flap and stepover, but his speciality is the rainbow flick. And in front of goal, his cheeky, fearless finishes are a joy to watch.

NEYMAR'S STATS

Finishing	92
Headers	86
Power	84
Speed	95
Dribbling	97
Creativity	94
Long Shots	94
Tricks	98
Footy Brain	88

MSN IN NUMBERS

MESSI

GAMES: 48 GOALS: 41
GOALS PER GAME: 0.85
ASSISTS: 24 HAT-TRICKS: 3

SUAREZ

GAMES: 53 GOALS: 59
GOALS PER GAME: 1.1
ASSISTS: 22 HAT-TRICKS: 8

NEYMAR

GAMES: 49 GOALS: 31
GOALS PER GAME: 0.63
ASSISTS: 20 HAT-TRICKS: 1

WHAT THE EXPERTS THINK

"With the three players we have up front, anything is possible!"
Rafinha, team-mate

"It is a pleasure to play alongside phenomena like Leo and Neymar!"
Luis Suarez
SOURCE: CANAL +

"It is a fantastic trio. They win games and do it well. It's really enjoyable to watch them!"
Paco Jemez
Granada manager
SOURCE: ESPORTES COPE

"The trident formed by Leo Messi, Neymar and Luis Suarez is the best trio in Barcelona's history!"
Edmilson, Former Barcelona defender

"For me, it is an honour to play alongside Messi and Suarez. Messi is the best friend I have!"
Neymar
SOURCE: CANAL +

BARCELONA STAT ATTACK!

Amazing stats and records from the Catalan club!

24

Barcelona have won La Liga a massive 24 times, which is second only to arch-rivals Real Madrid, and have finished runners-up 24 times as well!

6

After their 2015-16 league triumph, it means Barcelona have won six out of the last eight La Liga titles!

9

Chelsea's Pedro holds the record for the fastest hat-trick from a Barcelona player - he hit a 9-minute treble against Getafe back in 2013-14!

896

Former goalkeeper Victor Valdes went an amazing 896 minutes without conceding a goal in all competitions during the 2011-12 season!

The club have won the Copa del Rey an incredible 28 times, which is a record in Spain!
28
3
Last season, Luis Suarez became only the third player to hit 40 La Liga goals in one season after Lionel Messi and Cristiano Ronaldo!
767
Barça legend Xavi holds the record for the most games for the club, racking up 767 appearances in all competitions!
CAMPEONES 2016
CAMPEONATO DE ESPAÑA COPA DE S.M. EL REY
QATAR AIRWAYS
75
Lionel Messi holds the record for the most goals scored in one season – he hit an incredible 73 goals in all official comps in 2011-12!
In 2012-13, Barça finished on 100 points as they won La Liga, which is a record!
100
Qatar Foundation

GUIDE TO THE NOU CAMP

TURN OVER FOR STADIUM TOUR

GUIDE TO THE NOU CAMP

INSIDE THE STADIUM

▶ From inside the tunnel, players can hear the roar of thousands of fans, and the traditional club hymn, *'Cant del Barça'*.

▶ Inside the tunnel, and just a few metres from pitchside, is the Barcelona chapel. It is often visited by players before a big game.

▶ The chapel was built in 1958, not long after the ground itself was finished.

DRESSING ROOMS

▶ Barça's dressing room is divided into a changing space, a technical area, a wet area, and a space for medical treatment.

▶ In the technical area there are three offices, a meeting room, and a coaches' changing room.

▶ The wet area contains a swimming pool, two jacuzzis, a sauna, a steam room and an ice bath – perfect for relaxing after a tough match!

THE MUSEUM

▶ The Club Museum opened in 1984, and is one of the most popular tourist attractions in the whole of Barcelona.

▶ It contains trophies, memorabilia, and other famous items from the club's 115-year history.

▶ All five of Lionel Messi's Ballon d'Or awards are kept in the museum too, in an area dedicated to the Barcelona legend.

TROPHIES

- Barcelona have won 128 trophies, and you can check them out in the Nou Camp trophy room!
- Their trophy haul includes a number of titles that no longer exist, like the Inter-Cities Fairs Cup and the Catalan Football Championship.
- After their fifth Champions League win in 2015, Barça were allowed to keep the trophy and it is now on show in the trophy room!

MEDIA ROOMS

- This is where the world's media gather to grill Barcelona's players and manager after a game!
- Barça's press room (right) is named after former general secretary Ricard Maxenchs and has space for 135 journalists!
- The press box (above left) has 192 desks, two TV studios and 28 radio cabins, offering reporters a perfect view of the pitch.

THE CLUB SHOP

- Next to the stadium is Barça's club shop, selling more than 3,000 different products.
- The two-storey shop is one of the biggest stores in Europe, and offers everything from cuddly toys to shirt printing facilities.
- Last season, more than three million Barça shirts were sold worldwide - that's more than any other club on the planet!

THE NOU CAMP NOU

In 2017, 50 years on from its first ever game, work will begin on the redevelopment of the Nou Camp. The changes will help to create a massively improved experience for fans: for the first time, every single seat will be covered by a roof, while the bottom tier will be rebuilt to improve spectators' view of the pitch. Within five years, Barça's grand old stadium will be fit for the 21st Century.

£82.5 MILLION

Cost of the naming rights for the new Camp Nou

2021

The ground will be completed in February 2021

CREIEM EN
ELS SOMNIS

DID YOU KNOW?

The Nou Camp is the biggest football stadium in Europe!

£495 MILLION

Total cost of the redevelopment

105,000

The stadium's new capacity

BEFORE THEY WERE FAMOUS!

The crazy pictures Barcelona's stars don't want you to see!

LIONEL MESSI

2005

IVAN RAKITIC

2005

20 QUESTIONS

How much do you know about the Spanish Champions?

1 In which year was the Spanish club formed – 1888, 1899, 1903 or 1905?

2 In which year did they move into their Nou Camp home – 1907, 1937 or 1957?

3 How many La Liga titles has the club won – 23, 24, 25 or 26?

4 Which Barcelona superstar is also their all-time record goalscorer?

5 Which current player is also the club's all-time record signing?

6 From which top Brazilian club did Barcelona sign superstar Neymar?

7 Which player holds the record for the most number of games played for the club?

8 How many times have Barcelona won the Champions League trophy?

9 What is the name of Barcelona's current first-team coach?

10 What is the name of Barcelona's current first-team captain?

11 From which club did Barcelona sign Samuel Umtiti last summer?

12 What is the capacity of the Nou Camp – 97,354, 99,354, 101,354 or 103,354?

13 Barcelona signed defender Gerard Pique from which English club?

14 Who was Barcelona's top scorer in La Liga during the 2015-16 season?

15 What nationality is Barcelona playmaker Ivan Rakitic?

16 In which year did Barcelona last fail to win La Liga?

17 True or False? Barcelona used to play in a green and yellow home kit.

18 Who did Barcelona beat in last year's Copa del Rey final?

19 What does Barcelona's motto, 'Mes Que Un Club', actually mean?

20 In which year did Barcelona legend Lionel Messi make his senior debut for the club?

FACE IN THE CROWD

Can you spot ten Barcelona legends in this picture? The players below are all there somewhere!

ANSWERS ON P60-61

LIONEL MESSI'S... CAREER IN

LA LIGA DEBUT
October 2004
A 17-year-old Messi makes his La Liga debut against city rivals Espanyol, coming on in the 82nd minute, and a new star is born!

FIRST BARCELONA GOAL
May 2005
Messi comes on as a second-half sub, and just a few minutes later, takes a pass from Ronaldinho before perfectly lobbing the Albacete keeper to open his La Liga account!

FIRST LA LIGA TITLE
May 2005
Leo wins his first La Liga title in his debut season! The Catalan club claim their first title in six years, with Messi scoring one goal from his seven games.

CHAMPO LEAGUE HEARTACHE
May 2006
Leo stars in the Champions League for Barcelona, but gets injured in the quarter-final against Chelsea and misses the rest of the campaign. Barça beat Arsenal in the final, but a distraught Messi decides not to collect his medal, a decision he later regrets.

PICTURES

Check out the best moments from the Barcelona star's amazing career!

CHAMPIONS LEAGUE HERO IN ROME

May 2009

Three years later, he gets to collect a Champions League winners' medal. He scores a rare header in a 2-0 win over Manchester United in Rome to give Barcelona their third ever Champions League win.

FOURTH BALLON D'OR IN A ROW

January 2013

In January 2013, Messi becomes the first player ever to win the Ballon d'Or award FOUR years in a row after scoring an incredible 91 goals in all competitions in 2012.

SCORES IN 21 GAMES IN A ROW

May 2013

On November 11, 2012, the Barça hero scores in their 4-2 win against Real Mallorca. He goes on to find the net in his next 20 games, against every single opponent in La Liga, before his run comes to an end in a 2-1 win over Atletico.

GOLDEN SHOE TREBLE WINNER

May 2013

The records continue to fall as, just a few months later, he becomes the first player to win the European Golden Shoe three years in a row after scoring an incredible 46 La Liga goals during the season!

BREAKS BARCA GOAL RECORD

March 2014

On March 16, the Barcelona wizard hits a hat-trick at home to Osasuna to become the club's record goalscorer. He beats the record of 369 goals, belonging to Paulinho Alcantara, which had stood for 87 years!

TOP SCORER IN LA LIGA HISTORY

November 2014

On November 22, a hat-trick in the 5-1 rout of Sevilla sees Messi become the top scorer in La Liga history! His first goal takes him level with Telmo Zarra's 251 goals, before a tap-in gives him the record outright. Another seals the hat-trick, and puts him into the record books yet again!

MESSI THE BALLON D'OR RECORD BREAKER

January 2016

The Barcelona legend claims an amazing fifth Ballon d'Or title, beating Real Madrid rival Cristiano Ronaldo into second place and Barça team-mate Neymar into third.

MORE GOAL MILESTONES

February 2016

On February 17, Messi scores his 300th La Liga goal in a 3-1 win at Sporting Gijon. A few days later, he hits both goals in Barça's 2-0 win over Arsenal in the CL, the second of which is the club's 10,000th goal in official competitions.

THE DOUBLE DOUBLE LANDED

May 2016

The Argentina star sets up both goals as Barça beat Sevilla 2-0 in extra-time in the Copa del Rey final, which seals a domestic trophy double for the second season running. In total, Messi ends with 41 goals and 23 assists in another memorable season.

BARCA STARS' CARS!

Check out the Barcelona stars' awesome rides...

FERRARI 458

Top Speed: 201 mph

Price: £725,000

BUGATTI VEYRON

Top Speed: 254 mph

Price: £1.4 million

MESSI
MASERATI GRANTURISMO S
Top Speed: 188 mph
Price: £108,000
SUAREZ
RANGE ROVER
RANGE ROVER SPORT
Top Speed: 162 mph
Price: £84,000
NEYMAR
S GO 3208
PORSCHE PANAMERA
Top Speed: 190mph
Price: £113,075
RAKITIC
AUDI A6
Top Speed: 146mph
Price: £45,255
ALBA
AUDI Q7 SUV
Top Speed: 134mph
Price: £79,790
BUSQUETS
AUDI A4
Top Speed: 130mph
Price: £26,350

It's been another incredible goalscoring season for Barcelona – they bagged 173 in all competitions! Here are the top ten from 2015-16!

QR CODE EXPLAINED

This is a QR code – simply scan it with your phone or tablet to watch each video clip on YouTube. Here's how to do it:

Download and install a free QR Code reader from the app or android store.

Hold your phone or tablet over the QR code and you'll be sent to the clip. Wicked!

10

LUIS SUAREZ

v Roma

Champions League, November 24

Suarez's second goal in this 6-1 demolition of the Italians was class! After a cross from Neymar was only half cleared, the Uruguayan thumped the ball into the bottom corner with a stunning volley to put the Catalans 3-0 up!

9

LIONEL MESSI
v Roma
Champions League, November 24

This goal sums up why MSN are the best attacking trio in football history. The passing, movement and understanding between the three players was world-class, and the beautiful chipped finish by Messi was the icing on the cake!

MUNIR EL HADDADI
v Vilanovense
Copa del Rey, October 28

Barcelona fans got a glimpse of the future as Munir ran riot with two goals. His second was the best, and began with a sublime pass from Adriano before a clever backheel from Sandro gave the wonderkid an open goal.

7

LUIS SUAREZ
v Real Sociedad
La Liga, 28 November

Iniesta began the move with a pass over the topfor Dani Alves, before the right-back's cross picked out Suarez. Then, it's all about the Uruguayan: with the ball behind him, he unleashes an epic scissor-kick past the goalkeeper!

6

ANDRES INIESTA
v Real Madrid
La Liga, 21 November

Even with Messi on the bench, Barça totally bossed this game. Iniesta, Rakitic and Neymar tied the Real defence in knots with their passing, before the skipper smashed the ball into the top corner from the edge of the penalty area!

5

DANI ALVES
v Vilanovense
Copa del Rey, 28 October

Barça love flowing, passing moves, but Dani Alves wasn't bothered about that when he scored here. Picking the ball up 35 yards out, the right-back thumped it into the top corner with a rocket right-foot shot – his last goal for the club!

4

JORDI ALBA
v Sevilla
Copa del Rey final, 22 May

Alba's name might have been on the scoresheet, but this was all about Messi. He picked up the ball just inside Sevilla's half, then produced an epic pass out of nowhere to give his left-back a simple finish and put Barça a goal up in the Copa final.

3

LUIS SUAREZ

v Celta Vigo

La Liga,
14 February

One of Barça's most famous goals will be remembered for years. With Messi standing over the penalty, the keeper dived to his left expecting a shot, but instead, Leo rolled the ball to his right for Suarez to complete his hat-trick!

2

LIONEL MESSI

v Espanyol

Copa del Rey,
6 January

Messi scored plenty of free-kicks last season, but this effort against city rivals Espanyol was the pick of the bunch. With the scores tied at 1-1, Leo fired in a spectacular, dipping strike that bounced off the crossbar on its way in!

1

NEYMAR

v Villarreal

La Liga,
8 November

Neymar produced a moment of magic that will go down as one of the best Nou Camp goals ever! After a perfect cross from Suarez, Neymar controlled the ball, flicked it over his head and his marker before firing a volley home!

DESIGN YOUR OWN BARCELONA KIT!

We love doodling new kits, and now we want you to do the same with Barça's home and away kit!

Check out some of Barcelona's best and craziest home and away kits below, and then get creative! Grab your coloured pens or pencils and design new home and away kits for the Catalan giants. Then send it to us, and the best will win a Barça shirt of their choice!

BEST KITS!

1992 - orange away kit

2008-09 - home kit

1998-99 - home kit

1980s - home kit

1999-2000 - home kit

2006-07 - home kit

CRAZY KITS!

2012-13 away kit

1996-97 away kit

2013-14 away kit

2016-17 away kit

WIN A SHIRT!
One lucky reader will win a Barcelona shirt of their choice! Just send a photocopy of this page with your kit designs – or your designs on a separate piece of paper – and details to: Barcelona Annual 2017 Design Your Own Kit, Media House, Lynch Wood, Peterborough, PE2 6EA. We'll pick our winner and send them their prize! Closing date: March 31, 2017.
Name:
Date of birth:
Address:
Mobile:
Shirt:
Size:

WORDFIT

Fit the members of Barcelona's 2015-16 squad into the grid!

Adriano	Halilovic	Messi	Rakitic	Tello
Alba	Iniesta	Montoya	Roberto	Ter Stegen
Bravo	Kaptoum	Munir	Samper	Turan
Busquets	Mascherano	Neymar	Song	Umtiti
Douglas	Masip	Pique	Denis Suarez	Vermaelen
Gumbau	Mathieu	Rafinha	Luis Suarez	Vidal

SPOT THE DIFFERENCE

Study these two pictures carefully and then see if you can find the ten differences between them!

ANSWERS ON P60-61

JOHAN CRUYFF 1947-2016

In March 2016, Barcelona, Holland and football in general lost one of their greatest heroes.

JOHAN: THE PLAYER

In 1973, Cruyff arrived at Barcelona as the world's most expensive player, and with two Ballon d'Ors under his belt. Expectations were high, and he didn't disappoint. After his debut in October, Barça didn't lose another game for the rest of the season and won their first La Liga title in 14 years. His dribbling, technique and finishing were all world-class, but it was his brain that made him a true great. Cruyff dictated games, roaming around the pitch to wherever he was needed, and putting himself at the centre of every attack. He stayed at the Nou Camp for five seasons, winning another Ballon d'Or, and changing the club forever.

Cruyff played 231 games for Barcelona and scored 86 goals

CRUYFF: THE MANAGER

As a manager, Cruyff followed the same route that he had taken as a player, moving to Barcelona from Ajax in 1988. During his eight seasons in charge, he transformed the club. His squad of legendary players – including Guardiola, Romario, Koeman and Stoichkov – were known as 'The Dream Team', and won the first European Cup in Barça's history as well as four league titles in a row. More importantly, he ensured that Barça's success would continue by helping to build La Masia – the youth system that has produced the likes of Valdes, Puyol, Busquets, Xavi, Iniesta and, of course, Messi.

TOTAL FOOTBALL

'Totaalvoetbal' was a style of football played by Ajax and Holland in the 1970s. The idea was that every player should be able to play in any position, rotate all over the pitch, and dominate possession with quick passing. When Cruyff arrived at Barcelona he brought Total Football with him, and laid the foundations for the style that Barça still play today.

THE CRUYFF TURN

These days, using the inside of your foot to drag the ball back and change direction is a move used in almost every game. Cruyff first introduced it to the world in 1974 while playing for Holland against Sweden, completely surprising his marker, and a new trick was born.

CRUYFF'S BARÇA HONOURS

AS A PLAYER:

LA LIGA (1): 1973-74
COPA DEL REY (1): 1977/78

AS A MANAGER:

EUROPEAN CUP (1): 1991-92
CUP WINNERS CUP (1): 1988-89
LA LIGA (4): 1990-91, 1991-92, 1992-93, 1993-94
COPA DEL REY (1): 1989-90
EUROPEAN SUPER CUP (1): 1992
SPANISH SUPER CUP (3): 1991, 1992, 1994

"HE HAS HAD THE BIGGEST INFLUENCE ON FOOTBALL OUT OF ANYONE IN THE WORLD – FIRST AS A PLAYER, THEN AS A COACH."

PEP GUARDIOLA

SOURCE: MARCA.COM

EL CLASICO

THE HISTORY

The first ever Clasico took place in Madrid in 1902, and the two teams have hated each other pretty much ever since. In the same way that Barcelona is 'Mes Que Un Club' ('More Than a Club'), their rivalry with Real Madrid is about much more than just football.

The cities have been enemies for over 100 years, and this spilled over into football. While Real Madrid became associated with the Spanish royal family and government, Barcelona were a symbol of Catalonian independence. The Clasico developed into a clash between Spain and Catalonia. For Barça and their fans, it gave them the chance to show opposition to the government.

The fact that the two teams are usually in direct competition adds to the rivalry. Between them they have won 56 La Liga titles, more than all the other teams put together, and 27 of the last 32. They are also the only Spanish clubs to win the European Cup, with 16 trophy wins between them. Combined with the off-the-pitch tension, it makes the Clasico the most intense and hard-fought game in world football today.

264 Total El Clasico matches

109 Barcelona Clasico wins

9 Cup final clashes

THE BIGGEST GAME IN WORLD FOOTBALL

458 Barcelona Clasico goals

156 Combined total of major trophies

400 MILLION TV viewers worldwide

TOP 5 MATCHES

REAL MADRID	0
BARCELONA	5

La Liga, 1974

Johan Cruyff inspired Barça to a 5-0 win in his first Clasico. The Dutchman danced through Real's defence to make it 2-0, before assisting another three.

BARCELONA	2
REAL MADRID	0

Copa del Rey Final, 1990

In seven Clasico Copa finals, Barça have only won twice. This was the second, as Cruyff bagged his first domestic trophy as manager of the club.

BARCELONA	5
REAL MADRID	0

La Liga, 1994

This was the Dream Team at their absolute best. Guardiola controlled the midfield, while Laudrup, Stoichkov and Romario ran riot up front.

REAL MADRID	2
BARCELONA	6

La Liga, 2009

Xavi, Messi and Iniesta were in full flow as Barça became the first team to score six times away from home in a Clasico, and all but secure the title.

REAL MADRID	0
BARCELONA	2

CL Semi-Final, 2011

Two moments of Messi magic fired Barça through. After an ace finish for 1-0, he dribbled through the Real defence to dump them out of the CL.

EL CLASICO

THE HEROES

JOHAN CRUYFF

Cruyff was a hero to Barça fans even before his 5-0 Clasico wins as both player and manager. His decision to turn down Real Madrid and sign for the club in 1974 made him a Nou Camp hero without even kicking a ball.

RONALDINHO

It takes a very special player to get a standing ovation at the Bernabeu while playing for Barça, but two solo goals from Ronaldinho brought the crowd to their feet in one of the most memorable Clasico moments.

XAVI

No Barcelona player has played against Real more times than Xavi, whose 42 Clasico games include a seven-game unbeaten streak in La Liga between 2008 and 2011, five goals, and some dominant performances.

LIONEL MESSI

Messi first played against Real Madrid in 2005, and has appeared in almost every Clasico since. His hat-trick at the Bernabeu in 2014 took his tally of Clasico goals to 21, making him the fixture's top goalscorer of all time, while he also has more assists in the clash than any other player.

THE PLAYERS

LUIS FIGO

Figo was a hero to Barcelona fans until 2000, when he moved to Real Madrid for a world record transfer fee despite insisting he would stay in Catalonia. On his return to the Nou Camp the crowd's anger was fierce, with phones, coins, and even a pig's head thrown at him from the stands.

THE VILLAINS

ALFREDO DI STEFANO

In 1953, Di Stefano was all set to join Barcelona, before Real smuggled him away from under their noses. Not only did he score a record 18 goals against Barcelona, he also became Real's greatest player of all time.

JOSE MOURINHO

Since leaving Barça's coaching staff in 2000, Mourinho has returned as manager of Chelsea, Inter Milan and Real Madrid. His negative football and touchline antics have made him one of the most hated Clasico figures ever.

CRISTIANO RONALDO

The only player to score in six Clasicos in a row has been a menace to Barça since he arrived in Spain, with 16 goals in 28 games. His annual Balon d'Or battles with Lionel Messi have only added to his unpopularity.

BARÇA'S STARS OF THE FUTURE

La Masia is one the greatest football academies in the world. Meet the latest batch of youngsters aiming to be the next Puyols, Xavis and Messis!

DENIS SUAREZ

Age: 22

Position: Attacking midfielder

Boots: Nike Magista Obra II

Plays like: Pedro

Suarez joined Barça this summer after originally signing from Man. City in 2013. In his first year, he played a key role in firing the 'B' team to third in the Segunda Division, and after another successful season on loan at Sevilla, he was sold to Villarreal in 2015. With five goals and 11 assists, he fired his new team to a Europa League quarter-final and 4th in La Liga, and convinced Barça to activate their buy-back agreement. His tricky dribbling and creative passing with either foot will make him a massive threat from any position.

WILFRID KAPTOUM

Age: 20 Position: Midfielder

Boots: Nike Hypervenom Phinish

Plays like: Andres Iniesta

2015-16 was a big season for Kaptoum. After establishing himself as a key man for Barça B, the midfielder made his first-team debut against Vilanovense in the Copa del Rey, before scoring his first goal against Valencia in the same competition. With his vision and quick feet, a La Liga debut is surely set to follow soon.

MUNIR EL HADDADI

Age: 20

Position: Forward

Boots: Adidas X 15 Primeknit

Plays like: Lionel Messi

Munir has already made an impression on Barça's first team, with eight goals in 26 games during 2015-16. The left-footer loves using his close control and trickery to run at defenders, and can play anywhere across the front three. In the summer of 2016, the club tied him down to a new three year deal, before loaning him to Valencia for more first team football. The future is bright for the Spanish wonderkid.

SERGI SAMPER

Age: 21 **Position:** Midfielder

Boots: Nike Magista Obra

Plays like: Sergio Busquets

Barça's greatest teams have been built around players that can control games, like Guardiola, Xavi, and Busquets. Samper, who penned a new deal in July, may have to wait for his opportunity at the Nou Camp, but he has the intelligence, positioning and passing ability to become Barcelona's next great midfielder.

CARLES ALENA

Age: 18 **Position:** Midfielder

The teenager went viral in November 2015 after an incredible solo goal against Roma in the UEFA Youth League.

GODSWILL EKPOLO

Age: 21 **Position:** Right-back

Ekpolo can play in central defence or midfield, but loves to use his power and pace to attack from full-back.

LEE SEUNG-WOO

Age: 17 **Position:** Forward

The pacy South Korean forward is one of the best teenagers in world football, and could make a big impact very soon.

DANI ROMERA

Age: 20 **Position:** Forward

The striker scored six goals in just twelve games for Barça B last season after joining the club from Almeria in January.

RODRIGO TARIN

Age: 20 **Position:** Centre-back

Tarin has been compared to first-team star Gerard Pique because of his physique and impressive ability to read the game.

GERARD GUMBAU

Age: 21 **Position:** Midfielder

At over six feet tall, the cultured left footer offers Barça's midfield something different, and made his debut in 2015.

Gerard Gumbau

2015-16 XI V

Barcelona's line-up last season was one of their best ever, but

CLAUDIO BRAVO

Bravo had big gloves to fill when he replaced Victor Valdes in 2014, but he's proved his worth with two La Liga titles!

DANI ALVES

With four Copas del Rey, six La Ligas and three Champions Leagues, the Brazilian leaves the Nou Camp as a true legend.

JAVIER MASCHERANO

Signed as a midfielder, the Argentina skipper has firmly established himself as one of La Liga's best ever centre-backs!

GERARD PIQUE

The centre-back is one of Barcelona and Spain's greatest defenders, and one of the most decorated players in world football.

JORDI ALBA

Released by Barcelona as a teenage winger, Alba returned to the club after Euro 2012 as one of the world's best left-backs.

SERGIO BUSQUETS

The world's best holding midfielder continues to dominate games with his crisp passing and brilliant positional sense.

IVAN RAKITIC

The Croatian played a key role in Barça's treble winning campaign, scoring the opener in the 2015 Champions League Final.

ANDRES INIESTA

Still going strong after 14 years at the club and an incredible 28 trophies, Iniesta is one of European football's true greats.

LEO MESSI

The five-time Ballon d'Or winner is Barça's all-time top goalscorer, and arguably the greatest player of all time.

LUIS SUAREZ

Suarez's huge £75 million transfer to Barcelona from Liverpool in 2014 completed the most lethal attacking trio ever.

NEYMAR

After Romario, Ronaldo and Ronaldinho, Neymar is the latest in a long line of Barça's samba stars – and he could become the best.

Bravo

Alves Mascherano Pique Alba

Busquets

Rakitic Iniesta

Messi Suarez Neymar

ALL-TIME XI

could it beat a dream team of former Champions League winners?

VICTOR VALDES

No keeper has played more games, kept more clean sheets, or won more trophies for Barcelona than the La Masia graduate.

ALBERT FERRER

The pacy right back played for his hometown club for ten years, and played a key role in the 1992 Champions League Final success.

CARLES PUYOL

Puyol's never-say-die defending was just as key to Barça's success as the beautiful football played ahead of him.

RONALD KOEMAN

The Everton manager was a stylish defender in his day, and smashed in Barça's winner at the 1992 European Cup Final.

ERIC ABIDAL

The French defender was a real fans' favourite at the Nou Camp, overcoming a liver tumour to lift the 2011 Champions League trophy.

PEP GUARDIOLA

Years before he became a managerial legend, Pep bossed Barcelona's midfield for more than ten years at his boyhood club.

XAVI

Xavi took on the Guardiola role in Barça's midfield, and went on to win absolutely everything for both club and country.

JOSE BAKERO

The attacking midfielder's injury-time winner in the second round of the 1992 European Cup made him a Barcelona legend.

DAVID VILLA

Spain's all-time record goal scorer secured the 2011 Champions League trophy with a beautiful finish at Wembley.

ETO'O

Barça fans quickly forgot about Eto'o's Real Madrid past as his goals fired them to their second Champions League in 2006.

RONALDINHO

Ronaldinho's ridiculous tricks and incredible skill made him Barça's most entertaining player ever, as well as one of the best.

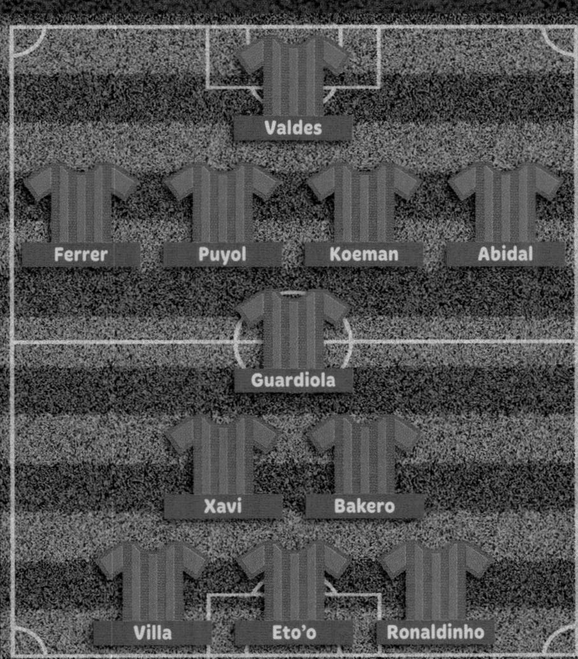

BARCELONA

FIRST TEAM SQUAD

2016-17

Check out the stars aiming to take Barcelona to more glory!

JASPER CILLESSEN

Position: Keeper **Country:** Holland

2015-16 La Liga apps/goals: N/A

Height: 185cm **Weight:** 83kg

MARC-ANDRE TER STEGEN

Position: Keeper **Country:** Germany

2015-16 La Liga apps/goals: 7/0

Height: 187cm **Weight:** 85kg

JORDI ALBA

Position: Defender **Country:** Spain

2015-16 La Liga apps/goals: 31/0

Height: 170cm **Weight:** 68kg

LUCAS DIGNE

Position: Defender **Country:** France

2015-16 La Liga apps/goals: N/A

Height: 178cm **Weight:** 74kg

DOUGLAS

Position: Defender **Country:** Brazil

2015-16 La Liga apps/goals: 1/0

Height: 171cm **Weight:** 67kg

JAVIER MASCHERANO

Position: Defender **Country:** Argentina

2015-16 La Liga apps/goals: 32/0

Height: 174cm **Weight:** 73kg

JEREMY MATHIEU

Position: Defender **Country:** France

2015-16 La Liga apps/goals: 21/0

Height: 189cm **Weight:** 84kg

GERARD PIQUE

Position: Defender **Country:** Spain

2015-16 La Liga apps/goals: 30/2

Height: 193cm **Weight:** 85kg

SAMUEL UMTITI

Position: Defender **Country:** France

2015-16 La Liga apps/goals: N/A

Height: 181cm **Weight:** 75kg

SERGIO BUSQUETS
Position: Midfielder **Country:** Spain
2015-16 La Liga apps/goals: 35/0
Height: 189cm **Weight:** 76kg

ANDRE GOMES
Position: Midfielder **Country:** Portugal
2015-16 La Liga apps/goals: 30/3
Height: 188cm **Weight:** 84kg

IVAN RAKITIC
Position: Midfielder **Country:** Croatia
2015-16 La Liga apps/goals: 36/7
Height: 184cm **Weight:** 78kg

ANDRES INIESTA
Position: Midfielder **Country:** Spain
2015-16 La Liga apps/goals: 28/1
Height: 171cm **Weight:** 68kg

RAFINHA
Position: Midfielder **Country:** Brazil
2015-16 La Liga apps/goals: 6/1
Height: 174cm **Weight:** 71kg

DENIS SUAREZ
Position: Midfielder **Country:** Spain
2015-16 La Liga apps/goals: 33/4
Height: 181cm **Weight:** 72kg

ARDA TURAN
Position: Midfielder **Country:** Turkey
2015-16 La Liga apps/goals: 18/2
Height: 178cm **Weight:** 76kg

ALEIX VIDAL
Position: Midfielder **Country:** Spain
2015-16 La Liga apps/goals: 9/0
Height: 178cm **Weight:** 69kg

SERGI ROBERTO
Position: Midfielder **Country:** Spain
2015-16 La Liga apps/goals: 31/0
Height: 178cm **Weight:** 71kg

LIONEL MESSI
Position: Forward **Country:** Argentina
2015-16 La Liga apps/goals: 33/26
Height: 170cm **Weight:** 72kg

NEYMAR
Position: Forward **Country:** Brazil
2015-16 La Liga apps/goals: 34/24
Height: 174cm **Weight:** 68kg

LUIS SUAREZ
Position: Forward **Country:** Uruguay
2015-16 La Liga apps/goals: 35/40
Height: 182cm **Weight:** 85kg

AND THE REST...

Jordi Masip
Position: Keeper
Country: Spain
Height: 180cm Weight: 69kg

Sergi Samper
Position: Midfielder
Country: Spain
Height: 181cm Weight: 71kg

Paco Alcacer
Position: Forward
Country: Spain
Height: 176cm Weight: 71kg

WORDSEARCH Page 14

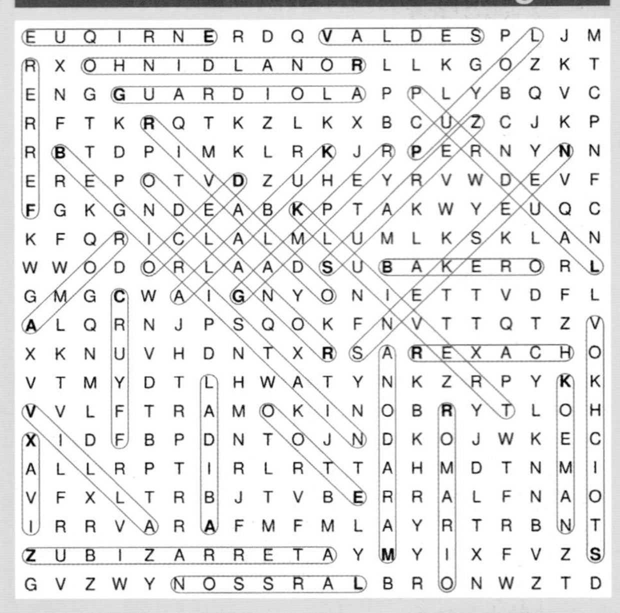

NAME THE TEAM Page 15

1. Marc-Andre Ter Stegen.
2. Javier Mascherano.
3. Jeremy Mathieu.
4. Ivan Rakitic.
5. Sergio Busquets.
6. Lionel Messi.
7. Dani Alves.
8. Neymar.
9. Andres Iniesta.
10. Luis Suarez.
11. Jordi Alba.

20 QUESTIONS Page 32

1. 1899; **2.** 1957; **3.** 24; **4.** Lionel Messi; **5.** Luis Suarez (officially); **6.** Santos; **7.** Xavi; **8.** Three; **9.** Luis Enrique; **10.** Andres Iniesta; **11.** Lyon; **12.** 99,354; **13.** Man. United; **14.** Luis Suarez; **15.** Croatian; **16.** 2014; **17.** False; **18.** Sevilla; **19.** More Than A Club; **20.** 2005.

FACE IN THE CROWD Page 33

WORDFIT Page 46

SON
ROBERTO
MUNIR
TER STEGEN
VERMAELEN
GUMBAU
BUSQUETS
TELLO
INIESTA
LUIS SUAREZ
DOUGLAS
MONTOYA
MASCHERANO
ADRIANO
MASIP
MESSI
TURAN
DENIS SUAREZ
UMTITI
SAMPER
HALILOVIC
ALBA
BRAVO
PIQUE
RAFINHA
VIDAL
KAPTOUM
RAKITIC
MATHIEU
NEYMAR

SPOT THE DIFFERENCE Page 47

1. Advertising hoarding has turned purple;
2. Ball has turned light blue;
3. Part of defender's boot has turned green;
4. Blue strip on defender's shirt;
5. White strip on defender's sock is now yellow;
6. La Liga badge on Alba's shirt has disappeared;
7. It reads QATAA instead of QATAR Airways;
8. Defender's head is missing;
9. Defender's shirt now has a Barcelona badge;
10. Alba's right foot is missing.

ROLL OF HONOUR

CHAMPIONS LEAGUE
991-92, 2005-06, 2008-09, 2010-11, 2014-15

FIFA CLUB WORLD CUP
2009-10, 2011-12, 2015-16

EUROPEAN CUP WINNERS' CUP
978-79, 1981-82, 1988-89, 1996-97

FAIRS CUP
957-58, 1959-60, 1965-66 (won outright in 1971)

EUROPEAN SUPER CUP
992-93, 1997-98, 2009-10, 2011-12, 2015-16

LATIN CUP
948-49, 1951-52

PYRENEES CUP
909-10, 1910-11, 1911-12, 1912-13

SPANISH LEAGUE CHAMPIONSHIP
928-29, 1944-45, 1947-48, 1948-49, 1951-52
952-53, 1958-59, 1959-60, 1973-74, 1984-85,
990-91, 1991-92, 1992-93, 1993-94, 1997-98,
998-99, 2004-05, 2005-06, 2008-09, 2009-10,
2010-11, 2012-13, 2014-158, 2015-16

SPANISH CUP
909-10, 1911-12, 1912-13, 1919-20, 1921-22,
924-25, 1925-26, 1927-28, 1941-42, 1950-51,
951-52, 1952-53, 1956-57, 1958-59, 1962-63,
967-68, 1970-71, 1977-78, 1980-81, 1982-83,
987-88, 1989-90, 1996-97, 1997-98,
2008-09, 2011-12, 2014-15, 2015-16

SPANISH SUPER CUP
983-84, 1991-92, 1992-93, 1994-95, 1996-97,
2005-06, 2006-07, 2009-10, 2010-11, 2011-12,
2013-14

SPANISH LEAGUE CUP
982-83, 1985-86

MEDITERRANEAN LEAGUE
937

CATALAN LEAGUE
937-38

CATALAN LEAGUE CHAMPIONSHIP
901-02, 1902-03, 1904-05, 1908-09, 1909-10,
910-11, 1912-13, 1915-16, 1918-19, 1919-20,
920-21, 1921-22, 1923-24, 1924-25, 1925-26,
926-27, 1927-28, 1929-30, 1930-31, 1931-32,
934-35, 1935-36, 1937-38 (includes Copa Macaya
(1901-02) and Copa Barcelona (1902-03)

CATALAN SUPER CUP
2014-15

CATALAN CUP
990-91, 1992-93, 1999-00, 2003-04, 2004-05,
2006-07, 2012-13, 2013-14 (until 1993-94, Copa
Generalitat)

EVA DUARTE CUP
948-49, 1951-52, 1952-53